Contents

The sunflower shown in this book grows in Europe, North America, Australia and Russia. A panel at the top of the pages shows when each stage in the sunflower's life cycle takes place. The sections on a yellow background give information about the life cycles of other types of plant.

Words in **bold** are explained in the glossary on page 30.

Time panel

Information about other flower species

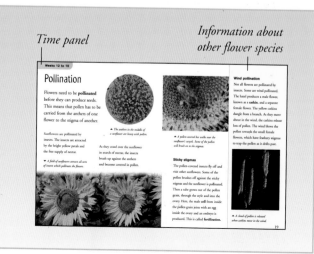

What is a sunflower?

A sunflower is a flowering plant. This means it produces flowers. The tallest sunflowers reach several metres in height, but some are smaller than this.

Plant parts

Most flowering plants have a shoot above ground and a root system below ground. The shoot is made up of **stems** and leaves. Like most plants, sunflowers have green leaves. The colour comes from a green chemical called **chlorophyll**. Plants use chlorophyll to make their own food by a process called **photosynthesis**.

◀ *Sunflowers are often grown as a crop. The plants contain oils.*

Life cycles

SUNFLOWERS
and other plants

Sally Morgan

Chrysalis Children's Books

First published in the UK in 2001 by

Chrysalis Children's Books

An imprint of Chrysalis Books Group Plc

The Chrysalis Building, Bramley Road,

London W10 6SP

Paperback edition first published in 2003

Copyright © Chrysalis Books Group Plc 2001

Editor: Russell McLean

Designer: Jacqueline Palmer

Educational consultant: Emma Harvey,
    Honeywell Infants School, London

ISBN 1 84138 309 0 (hb)

ISBN 1 84138 866 1 (pb)

Printed in Hong Kong

10 9 8 7 6 5 4 3 2 1 (hb)

10 9 8 7 6 5 4 3 2   (pb)

British Library Cataloguing in Publication Data
for this book is available from the British Library.

Picture acknowledgements:

G.I. Bernard/NHPA: 24l. Frank Blackburn/Ecoscene: 11tl, 11tr. Andrew Brown/
Ecoscene: 25t, 26b. Anthony Cooper/Ecoscene: 13b, 25c. Joel Creed/Ecoscene:
11b. Ecoscene: 25b. Chinch Gryniewicz/Ecoscene: 7r, 20, 26t, 29tl. Image Quest/
NHPA: 11cl. Alexandra Jones/Ecoscene: 9br. Genevieve Leaper/Ecoscene: 23br.
Sally Morgan/Ecoscene: 5cr, 5br, 7bl, 15bc, 16bl, 27cl. Graham Neden/Ecoscene:
28b. Papilio: front cover tr & c & bl, 1, 3tl, 4, 6tr, 15br, 19br, 21t, 23c, 29tc,
29c. Claire Paxton: 21br. Robert Pickett/Papilio: 18b, 29cl. K Preston-Mafham/
Premaphotos: 12l, 16tr, 23t. Roger Tidman/NHPA: 22bl. M. I. Walker/NHPA:
27br. Dave Wootton/Ecoscene: 28t.

All other photography by Robert Pickett.

Every attempt has been made to clear copyrights but should there be
inadvertent omissions please apply to the publisher for rectification.

flower

petal

leaf

stem

▲ _A sunflower has a shoot above ground._
The roots are hidden below ground.

Colourful flowers

Sunflowers usually produce large
yellow flowers during the summer,
when there are long days and short
nights. Some types of sunflower
have bronze or red-coloured **petals**.
The flowers turn into fruits that
contain seeds. The seeds drop
to the ground. In spring, they
grow into new plants.

The daisy family

Sunflowers belong to a large group
of flowering plants called daisies.
Other plants in this group include
daisies, dandelions, thistles and
cornflowers. Many of them grow in
gardens and have colourful flowers.

▶ _The flower of the globe_
thistle attracts bees.

▼ _Ox-eye daisies_
have a ring of white
petals around a
yellow disc.

The seed

The life cycle of a sunflower begins with a seed, which will grow into a new plant.

▲ *A sunflower seed is about 1 centimetre long.*

Inside a seed

A sunflower seed is oval shaped and has an outer covering called a seed coat, or **testa**. This is dry and hard, and it protects the **embryo** plant inside. The embryo will grow into the new plant.

The embryo is made up of a tiny shoot and root, with two seed leaves. The seed leaves are swollen with a food store of **fats** and **carbohydrates**. The embryo plant uses this food when it starts to grow.

◀ *Inside a seed, the swollen seed leaves take up most of the space.*

Eating seeds

Many seeds are good to eat. Peas, beans and lentils are cooked as vegetables. **Cereals** such as wheat, rye, maize and rice are the staple diet in many countries. They have seeds which are swollen with **starch**, a type of carbohydrate. Wheat seeds are made into flour, which is used to make bread. Most rice seeds have their seed coats removed to leave a shiny white grain of starch. This is sold as white rice. A rice seed with its seed coat left in place is called brown rice. The rice has to be cooked before it can be eaten.

▲ *Peas, beans and lentils can be dried and stored for future use.*

▶ *Cereals such as wheat are high-energy foods.*

Beginning to grow

Many seeds can survive in the ground for months, even years. When the conditions are right, a seed starts to grow. The growth of a seed into a **seedling** is called **germination**.

▲ *A young root emerges from the seed and grows downwards.*

A sunflower seed needs water, warmth and air before it will germinate. First, the seed takes up a lot of water. It swells and the seed coat splits open. After a few days a young root, called a **radicle**, appears. The radicle grows down into the ground and anchors the seed in place. Then a young shoot pushes upwards, out of the soil.

▶ *The shoot pushes out of the seed coat and grows towards the surface.*

▲ *The shoot pulls the seed leaves out of the seed.*

▲ *The shoot straightens and the seed leaves open.*

The growing tip of the shoot is protected between two seed leaves. These open out of the seed coat. The seed leaves are small, round and fat. Once the food in the seed leaves has been used up, they drop off.

◀ *The seedling uses the food stored in its seed leaves to grow.*

The right conditions

A seed germinates only when the conditions are right. This gives the young plant the best chance of surviving. Many tree seeds germinate after frosty weather. This makes sure that the seeds germinate in spring and not autumn. Some seeds germinate only after a fire. They have a thick seed coat which is not harmed by the heat. When they germinate, all the other plants have been burnt, so the seeds can use all the rich **nutrients** in the ash left by the fire.

▼ *This banksia seedling germinated after a fire. You can see the ash on the ground.*

Leaves and stems

After a week or so, the young stem is several centimetres tall and the first true leaves have appeared.

◀ The first true leaves appear at the tip of the stem.

The leaves of a sunflower are thin, flat and heart-shaped. Each one is attached to the main stem by a short stem called a **petiole**. The leaves are spaced evenly up the stem, in pairs. This is the best position to catch the sunlight which the sunflower needs to make food. As the sunflower grows, new leaves form at the tip.

The stem is very hairy. Insects don't like the hairs and this stops them from landing on the plant and eating the leaves.

◀ Fine hairs completely cover the stem.

◀ The stem of a sunflower has to be quite sturdy to support all the leaves.

▲ *A field maple leaf has wavy edges.*

▲ *Ash leaflets grow in pairs.*

▼ *A giant Amazon water lily leaf in Brazil.*

Leaf shapes

Leaves are many different shapes. The oak tree has a simple leaf with wavy edges. A holly leaf has spikes along its edge to stop animals eating it. **Compound** leaves, such as a horse chestnut leaf, are made up of many **leaflets**. The leaf of an ash tree is made up of leaflets which grow in pairs along a central stem.

▲ *The five leaflets of a horse chestnut leaf.*

The giant Amazon water lily has one of the largest leaves. The huge discs grow up to two metres across and float on the surface of ponds and lakes. They have ribs that run out from the centre, like spokes on a wheel. The leaves are so strong that small animals can stand on them.

Growing tall

Plants grow up towards the Sun so that as much light as possible falls on their leaves. Sunflowers grow taller than many plants, so they get more light.

Making food

Sunflowers and most other plants make their own food in their leaves and green stems. This process is called photosynthesis. The plant needs sunlight, **carbon dioxide** gas from the air and water from the soil. The carbon dioxide enters the leaves through tiny holes, or **pores**, called **stomata**. The water enters the roots and is carried to the leaves.

◀ *The tallest sunflowers reach a height of up to 3 metres.*

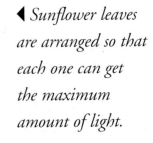

◀ *Sunflower leaves are arranged so that each one can get the maximum amount of light.*

▼ *Photosynthesis takes place in the green stems and leaves.*

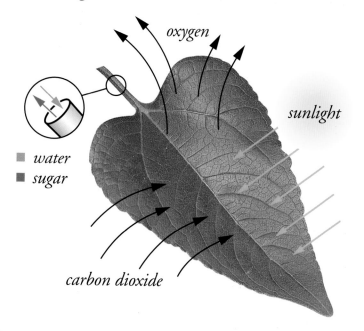

oxygen

sunlight

■ water
■ sugar

carbon dioxide

Photosynthesis

Photosynthesis takes place during daylight. The light gives the sunflower energy which it uses to join together the carbon dioxide and the water to make sugar and a gas called **oxygen**. The sunflower uses the sugar to grow. Some of the sugar is changed into starch and stored for use in the future. The oxygen is released into the air.

Evergreen or deciduous?

Some trees drop their leaves in autumn or during the dry season. The leaves turn yellow and red and then drop off. The trees grow new leaves at the beginning of the next growing season. These plants are called **deciduous**.

The holly is an **evergreen** plant because it keeps its leaves all year round. Evergreen leaves are often shiny because they are covered in a layer of wax. This helps the plant to **conserve** its water during cold weather.

◀ *Deciduous trees drop their leaves by winter. Evergreen trees keep their leaves all year round.*

Underground roots

The roots of a plant hold it firmly in the ground and take up water. A sunflower has a network of roots that spread through the soil.

The roots of a sunflower are fibrous. This means they are long and fine. At the tip of each root is a mass of tiny threads called root hairs. The root hairs make the surface area of the root bigger, so that it can take up more water.

The water is carried through the roots and stem up to the leaves. The water contains nutrients which the sunflower needs to stay healthy.

▼ *Sunflower roots spread out through the top layer of the soil.*

Wilting leaves

If a sunflower does not have enough water, its leaves **wilt**. This means they become floppy. They soon recover if they are given water. But if the leaves are allowed to wilt for too long, they shrivel up and die.

◀ *Floppy leaves are a sign that a plant needs water.*

Root types

Some plants, such as the dandelion, poppy and dock, have a single large root called a **tap root**. The tap root grows straight down into the soil, with smaller roots branching off it. It is swollen with stored food.

In autumn, a dahlia's roots become swollen with food and form **tubers**. The rest of the plant dies, but the tubers survive the winter underground. In spring, the plant uses the food in the tubers to grow.

▶ *A dandelion (far right) has a single tap root. A dahlia (right) has many tubers.*

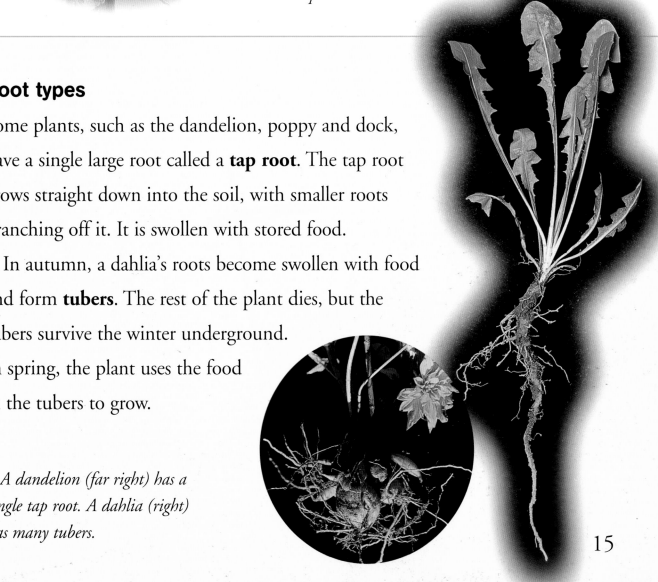

15

The flower

Flowers range from tiny green ones to brightly-coloured blooms that nobody can miss. Their job is to produce seeds.

▲ *The petals of a daffodil join together in a tube.*

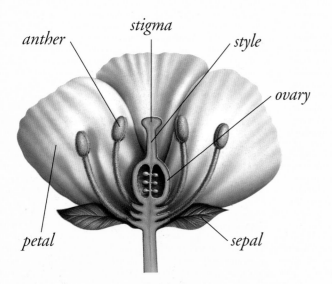

anther stigma style ovary petal sepal

▲ *The parts of a typical flower.*

▼ *The anthers of this lily are covered with powdery yellow pollen.*

Flower parts

Most flowers have a ring of petals which are brightly coloured to attract insects. The petals may be separate or joined together to form a tube. At the bottom of the petals are tiny cups called **nectaries**. They make a sugary **nectar** which insects love. The male parts of the flower are called **stamens**. Each stamen ends in an **anther** which produces **pollen**. The female parts are the **carpels**. A carpel is made up of a **stigma**, a **style** and an **ovary**.

Mini-flowers

Sunflowers belong to the daisy family.
Daisy flowers are quite complex.
Each flower head is really made
up of lots of mini-flowers, or **florets**.
The florets around the edge each have
one large, single petal. The florets in
the middle do not have petals. They
have either stamens or carpels instead.

▲ *The **bud** of a sunflower is made
up of many green **sepals** which
cover and protect the petals.*

▶ *The sepals open to make a
green ring around the flower.
The yellow petals begin to unfurl.*

◀ *The flower is fully open.
A ring of large petals surrounds
the stamens. The anthers are
covered in pollen. The carpels
are hidden in the middle.*

17

Pollination

Flowers need to be **pollinated** before they can produce seeds. This means that pollen has to be carried from the anthers of one flower to the stigma of another.

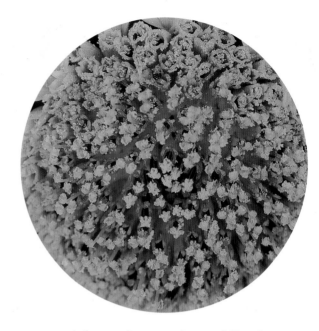

▲ *The anthers in the middle of a sunflower are heavy with pollen.*

Sunflowers are pollinated by insects. The insects are attracted by the bright yellow petals and the free supply of nectar.

▼ *A field of sunflowers attracts all sorts of insects which pollinate the flowers.*

As they crawl over the sunflower in search of nectar, the insects brush up against the anthers and become covered in pollen.

▲ *A pollen-covered bee walks over the sunflower's carpels. Some of the pollen will brush on to the stigmas.*

Sticky stigmas

The pollen-covered insects fly off and visit other sunflowers. Some of the pollen brushes off against the sticky stigmas and the sunflower is pollinated. Then a tube grows out of the pollen grain, through the style and into the ovary. Here, the male **cell** from inside the pollen grain joins with an egg inside the ovary and an embryo is produced. This is called **fertilization.**

Wind pollination

Not all flowers are pollinated by insects. Some are wind pollinated. The hazel produces a male flower, known as a **catkin**, and a separate female flower. The yellow catkins dangle from a branch. As they move about in the wind, the catkins release lots of pollen. The wind blows the pollen towards the small female flowers, which have feathery stigmas to trap the pollen as it drifts past.

▲ *A cloud of pollen is released when catkins move in the wind.*

Fruits and seeds

When a sunflower has been pollinated and fertilized, the flower head bends over, the petals drop off and the anthers wither. Then the seeds start to develop.

Forming fruit

The ovaries of a sunflower become much larger once they have been fertilized. The embryo plants begin to grow inside them. After a week or so, each embryo is made up of a tiny shoot and root, with two seed leaves. The seed leaves swell as the sunflower transports food to its ovaries. The walls of each seed dry out and harden to form a seed coat. At the same time, the walls of the ovaries become drier as they turn into fruits. The seeds are ready to be scattered.

▲ *The petals and anthers have dropped off this sunflower. You can see the ovaries of the flower, where the seeds form.*

Fruit or seed?

We think of fruits as being sweet-tasting and good to eat, but some fruits are hard, dry or prickly.

A real fruit forms from the ovary of a flower. The seeds are inside the fruit. A plum has a thick, fleshy layer that tastes sweet. This is the fruit. In the middle is a hard, brown stone which contains the seed. The pod of a bean or a pea is a fruit, too. The seeds are the beans and peas inside the pod.

▲ *A strawberry is not a true fruit.*

False fruits

A strawberry is not a proper fruit, because its flesh forms from the base of the flower, not the ovary. The fruits are the tiny triangular bits stuck on the outside. Inside each of these tiny fruits is an even smaller seed. An apple is a false fruit, too. The fleshy part of the apple is the swollen base of the flower. The real fruit is the core which contains the seeds.

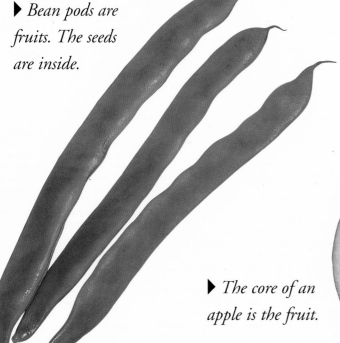

▶ *Bean pods are fruits. The seeds are inside.*

▶ *The core of an apple is the fruit.*

Scattering seeds

Plants have many ways of making sure that their seeds are carried far away. They use animals, wind and even water to scatter their seeds.

Eaten by birds

In the autumn, as the heads of the sunflowers dry up and the seeds ripen, flocks of seed-eating birds land on the flowers to pick out the seeds.

▲ *When the flower head is dry, the seeds fall to the ground easily.*

Many of the seeds are eaten by the birds, but some fall to the ground. Others are dropped by the birds as they fly away. These seeds survive the winter in the soil and then germinate in spring.

◀ *Tits and finches perch on old flower heads and eat the seeds.*

▶ Sycamore seeds have wings which carry them away from the tree.

Parachutes and catapults

Flowers such as the dandelion produce fruits with hairy parachutes that catch the wind. Some plants have pods that act like catapults. When the pods dry out, they split open and sling the seeds far away.

▲ The wind will scatter these dandelion seeds.

Birds and mammals eat tasty berries. The seeds inside the berries pass through the animal's gut and are scattered in its droppings. Small mammals, such as squirrels and voles, bury hazelnuts and acorns as a source of food for the winter. Often they forget where these fruits are hidden. The seeds survive and germinate in spring.

▶ Broom seeds are scattered when the pods dry out and split open.

Life span

There are three names to describe how long a plant lives – annual, biennial and perennial. Sunflowers are annuals.

Annuals

A sunflower is an annual because it lives for one growing season. The seed grows into an adult plant within four or five months. It flowers, sets seed and dies by autumn.

A dead sunflower is broken down by animals, **fungi** and **bacteria** that feed on dead plants and animals. This process is called **decomposition**. The nutrients are returned to the soil where they can be used by other plants.

◀ *By late autumn, a sunflower's leaves are dying and its seeds have been scattered.*

Biennials

Biennial plants live for two growing seasons. They grow through the first year, survive the winter and flower in their second season. Foxgloves and hollyhocks are biennials.

▲ *Foxgloves flower in their second year, release lots of seeds and then die.*

Perennials

Perennials live for many years. At the end of each summer, their shoots die back and by winter nothing can be seen above ground. But their roots survive, and in spring they produce new shoots.

Woody perennials

These plants have woody stems. The stems do not die back, but live for many years. Each year they produce new growth from the shoot tips. They grow into shrubs and trees.

▶ *Ferns are perennials. They grow new **fronds** in spring.*

▼ *Trees and shrubs are woody perennials. They can live for many years.*

Plant types

There are more than 380 000 types of plants in the world. They range in size from tiny **algae** to giant redwood trees.

▲ *Wheat (above), rice and barley are all grasses.*

Flowering plants

This large group of plants includes cacti, grasses, flowers that grow from **bulbs** and even meat-eating plants.

Cacti Cacti can survive in deserts where it may not rain for many years. Their stems are covered in a thick wax layer to conserve water. Their roots often cover a large area, to take up as much water as possible when it rains.

Grasses Grasses have long, thin leaves. They produce small green flower spikes which release lots of pollen. Grass pollen gives many people hayfever in summer.

Bulb-producing flowers These plants include tulips and daffodils. At the end of summer the leaves die back. All that is left is a bulb – an underground food store. A bulb is not the same as a root. It is formed from the swollen base of the leaves. In spring, the bulb produces new shoots and flowers.

◄ *Cacti have spines instead of leaves, to stop animals from eating them.*

Carnivorous plants

These plants eat animals! The leaves of a pitcher plant are shaped like a jug with a lid. Each jug is filled with water. When a fly crawls into a jug, it slips down into the water and dies. Its body is broken down into nutrients which are taken up by the leaf.

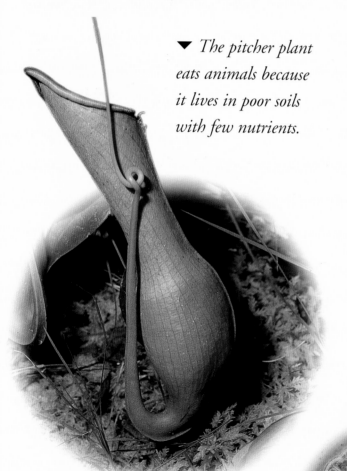

▼ *The pitcher plant eats animals because it lives in poor soils with few nutrients.*

▶ *The structure of this alga can only be seen under a microscope.*

Trees

Trees belong to many different families, but they all have thick, woody stems. The wood supports the tree and allows it to grow much larger than other plants. **Coniferous** trees have needle-shaped leaves and cones instead of flowers. Deciduous broad-leaved trees have leaves which are wide and thin.

Non-flowering plants

These include algae, mosses and ferns. Algae are simple plants which do not have roots, stems or leaves. They range from microscopic green algae to huge seaweeds. Mosses have simple leaves, while ferns have leaf-like fronds. Both mosses and ferns live in damp, shady places, as their leaves lose water easily.

Amazing plants

◀ *The stinking rafflesia grows on the floor of rainforests.*

- The largest flower belongs to the rafflesia, which grows in Southeast Asia. The flower is more than one metre across and weighs up to 11 kg. It stinks of rotting meat, which attracts flies. The flies crawl inside the flower and pollinate it.

- The smallest flowers are produced by floating duckweed. The whole plant is just 0.6 mm long.

- The largest seed in the world is produced by the coco-de-mer, a giant fan palm in the Seychelles. The heart-shaped fruit weighs 20 kg and takes as long as ten years to form.

- The giant redwoods and bristle cone pines of North America can live for more than 5000 years. The redwoods grow to a great size. The most massive tree in the world is a giant redwood called the General Sherman, in California. It is 83.8m tall and measures 31m around its trunk.

- The welwitschia of Namibia may live for 100 years or more. It only has two leaves, which grow a few centimetres each year. Some of the oldest leaves are more than 8m long.

▼ *The two leaves of a welwitschia split many times in the dry and windy desert climate.*

The life cycle of a sunflower

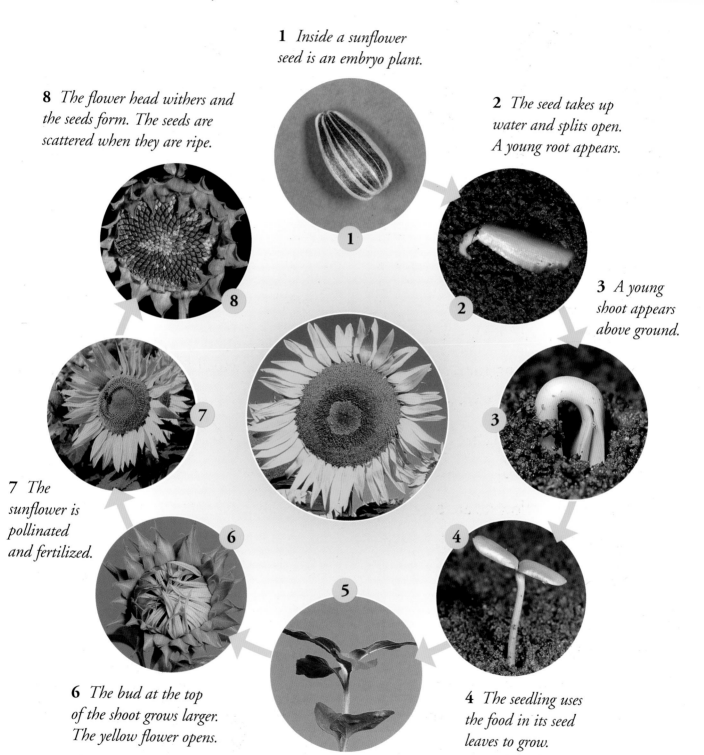

1 *Inside a sunflower seed is an embryo plant.*

8 *The flower head withers and the seeds form. The seeds are scattered when they are ripe.*

2 *The seed takes up water and splits open. A young root appears.*

3 *A young shoot appears above ground.*

7 *The sunflower is pollinated and fertilized.*

6 *The bud at the top of the shoot grows larger. The yellow flower opens.*

4 *The seedling uses the food in its seed leaves to grow.*

5 *The shoot grows quickly. True leaves appear in pairs.*

Glossary

algae Simple plants that are mainly found in water, ranging from microscopic organisms to huge seaweeds.

anther A male part of a flower that produces pollen.

bacteria Microscopic organisms that have only one cell.

bud A leaf or flower before it opens.

bulb An underground store of food made from leaves that can grow into a new plant.

carbohydrate A high-energy food substance that is often stored in plant roots and seeds.

carbon dioxide A colourless gas in the air. Plants use it in photosynthesis.

carpel A female part of a flower, made up of a stigma, a style and an ovary.

catkin The male flower of a plant such as the willow, hazel or birch.

cell One of the tiny building blocks that make up a living organism.

cereal A grass that produces grains which can be eaten, such as wheat, rice, oats and barley.

chlorophyll A green chemical in plants.

compound Made up of two or more parts joined together.

coniferous Producing cones instead of flowers. Pines and firs are coniferous trees.

conserve To keep.

deciduous Shedding leaves in autumn or at the end of the growing season.

decomposition The process of breaking down a dead plant or animal.

embryo The young plant inside a seed, or an animal in its earliest stage of growth.

evergreen A shrub or tree that bears leaves all year round, such as the holly or the pine.

fat A food substance that is high in energy.

fertilization In a plant, the joining together of a male pollen cell and a female egg to form an embryo in a seed.

floret A small flower. The head of a sunflower is made up of many florets.

frond The leaf of a fern.

fungus (plural **fungi**) An organism that is neither animal nor plant. Most fungi are made up of tiny threads that grow through soil.

germination The growth of a seed into a seedling.

leaflet A small leaf that makes up part of a compound leaf.

nectar Sweet, sticky liquid made by flowers to attract insects.

nectary A pouch at the base of a petal that produces nectar.

nutrient Chemicals that plants and animals need for healthy growth.

ovary The female part of a flower that contains the egg.

oxygen A colourless gas in the air. Most plants and animals need oxygen to live.

petal A part of a flower that is often brightly coloured to attract birds and insects.

petiole The stalk of a leaf.

photosynthesis The way plants use light to change water and carbon dioxide into sugar, which they use as food, and oxygen.

pollen Yellow, powdery grains produced by the anthers of a flower.

pollinate To move pollen from the anther of one flower to the stigma of another.

pore A tiny opening.

radicle The young root produced by a seed.

seedling A very young plant.

sepals Green flaps, like petals, that protect a flower before it opens.

stamen A male part of a flower, made up of an anther supported on a filament, or stalk.

starch A type of carbohydrate.

stem The main stalk of a plant.

stigma The tip of a flower's carpel that receives the pollen.

stomata Tiny pores in a leaf which allow gases to enter and leave the leaf.

style The long, slim middle part of a carpel.

tap root The main root of some plants that is swollen with food.

testa The seed coat.

tuber A swollen part of a root that stores food for the growing plant.

wilt To lose support and become floppy.

Index